First World War
and Army of Occupation
War Diary
France, Belgium and Germany

14 DIVISION
43 Infantry Brigade
Highland Light Infantry
10th (Service) Battalion
1 June 1918 - 13 June 1919

WO95/1910/1

The Naval & Military Press Ltd
www.nmarchive.com
Published in association with The National Archives

Published by

The Naval & Military Press Ltd

Unit 10 Ridgewood Industrial Park,

Uckfield, East Sussex,

TN22 5QE England

Tel: +44 (0) 1825 749494

www.naval-military-press.com

www.nmarchive.com

This diary has been reprinted in facsimile from the original. Any imperfections are inevitably reproduced and the quality may fall short of modern type and cartographic standards.

© Crown Copyright
Images reproduced by permission of The National Archives, London, England, 2015.

Contents

Document type	Place/Title	Date From	Date To
Heading	WO95/1910/1 14 Div-43 Inf Bde 10 Highland Light Inf Jan 1918-Jan 1919		
Heading	14th Division 43rd Infy Bde 10th Bn Highland Lt Infy Jun 1918-Jun 1919		
Heading	Vol 34 10th Highland Light Infantry War Diary For June 1918		
War Diary	Esquelbecq	01/06/1918	03/06/1918
War Diary	Rety	04/06/1918	12/06/1918
War Diary	Brunembert	13/06/1918	16/06/1918
War Diary	Boulogne	17/06/1918	17/06/1918
War Diary	Brookwood	18/06/1918	21/06/1918
War Diary	Pirbright	22/06/1918	30/06/1918
Heading	Vol 35 10th High. L. I. War Diary For July 1918.		
Miscellaneous	Cover for Documents. Nature of Enclosures.		
War Diary	Bullswater Camp Pirbright.	01/07/1918	04/07/1918
War Diary	Folkestone	05/07/1918	05/07/1918
War Diary	Boulogne	06/07/1918	06/07/1918
War Diary	Mesnil	07/07/1918	11/07/1918
War Diary	Alembon.	12/07/1918	12/07/1918
War Diary	Tournehem	13/07/1918	13/07/1918
War Diary	Nortleilinghem.	14/07/1918	29/07/1918
War Diary	Tatinghem	30/07/1918	30/07/1918
War Diary	Staple	31/07/1918	31/07/1918
Heading	10th (S) Bn. High. LI. War Diary For August. 1918 Vol 36		
Miscellaneous	Cover For Documents. Nature Of Enclosures.		
War Diary	27/w/a1.9 Near Caestre.	01/08/1918	16/08/1918
War Diary	Droglandt	17/08/1918	17/08/1918
War Diary	Proven	18/08/1918	18/08/1918
War Diary	Orillia Camp Vlamertinghe	19/08/1918	23/08/1918
War Diary	Bibstay Castle Vlamertinghe H.11.b.8.3	24/08/1918	27/08/1918
War Diary	Ypres I.14.b.1.9	28/08/1918	31/08/1918
War Diary	Ypres	28/08/1918	31/08/1918
War Diary			
War Diary	Confidential Vol 40 War Diary of 10th High. L.I. For September 1918		
Heading	Training		
War Diary	Front Line Ypres Sector Bn. HQ. I.14.b.1.9.	01/09/1918	01/09/1918
War Diary	Vlamertinghe	02/09/1918	06/09/1918
War Diary	Bde. Support Area Bn. HQ. Bobstay Castle	07/09/1918	11/09/1918
War Diary	Front Line Ypres Sector Bn.HQ. I14b.1.9.	12/09/1918	14/09/1918
War Diary	School Camp St. Jan Ter Biezen	16/09/1918	20/09/1918
War Diary	Front Line Bn. HQ. H24c 5.3. (Sheet 28)	21/09/1918	25/09/1918
War Diary	Steenvoorde	26/09/1918	26/09/1918
War Diary	Dominion Camp G 24 A (Sheet 28)	27/09/1918	27/09/1918
War Diary	In Action	28/09/1918	29/09/1918
War Diary	Pioneer Camp H 21b.4.7.	30/09/1918	30/09/1918
Heading	10th H.L.I. War Diary October 1918		
Heading	Cover for Documents. BM/234 Natures Of Enclosures. C.O.		

War Diary	Pioneer Camp	01/10/1918	01/10/1918
War Diary	Potijze	02/10/1918	11/10/1918
War Diary	Wulverghem Area & Messines	12/10/1918	14/10/1918
War Diary	Wervicq	15/10/1918	16/10/1918
War Diary	Wervicq & Roncq	17/10/1918	17/10/1918
War Diary	Roncq & Mouscron	18/10/1918	18/10/1918
War Diary	Mouscron	18/10/1918	18/10/1918
War Diary	Herseaux	19/10/1918	19/10/1918
War Diary	Trieu	20/10/1918	20/10/1918
War Diary	Quevaucamp	21/10/1918	31/10/1918
Heading	Vol 42 War Diary 10th Highland L.I. November 1918		
War Diary	Quevaucamp	01/11/1918	07/11/1918
War Diary	Helchin	08/11/1918	09/11/1918
War Diary	Ime De Naverie	10/11/1918	12/11/1918
War Diary	St Leger	13/11/1918	14/11/1918
War Diary	Tourcoing	15/11/1918	30/11/1918
Heading	10th High. L. I. Vol 43 War Diary For December 1918		
War Diary	Tourcoing	01/12/1918	31/12/1918
Heading	War Diary of 10th (S) Bn Highland Light Infantry For January 1919. Vol 44		
Miscellaneous	Cover for Documents. Nature of Enclosures.		
War Diary	Tourcoing	01/01/1919	03/01/1919
War Diary	Marcq	04/01/1919	31/01/1919
Heading	War Diary of 10th (S) Bn Highland Light Infantry From 1 February 1919 To 28th February 1919 Vol 45		
Miscellaneous	Cover For Documents. Nature Of Enclosures.		
War Diary	Marcq	01/02/1919	28/02/1919
Heading	War Diary 10th Bn Highland L. I. March 1919. Vol 46		
War Diary	Marcq	01/03/1919	26/03/1919
War Diary	Petit Oudenarde	27/03/1919	31/03/1919
Heading	War Diary For April 1919 Of 10th Bn. Highland Light Infantry. Vol 47		
Miscellaneous	Cover for Documents. Nature of Enclosures.		
War Diary	Petit Oudenarde	01/04/1919	30/04/1919
Heading	War Diary of 10th/11 High. L I. For May 1919. Vol 48		
Miscellaneous	Cover For Documents. Nature Of Enclosures.		
War Diary	Petit Audenarde	01/05/1919	31/05/1919
Heading	War Diary of 10th/11 Highland Light Infantry From 1st To 14th June 1919 Final		
War Diary	Petit Audenarde	01/06/1919	13/06/1919

WO95/1910-1

14 Div — 43 Inf Bde

10 Highland Light Inf

Jan 1918 — Jun 1919

14TH DIVISION
43RD INFY BDE

10TH BN HIGHLAND LT INFY

JUN 1918 – JUN 1919

FROM 15 DIV 46 BDE

Formerly 10/11 from 1916 May
to May 18 (15 Div) 46 BDE

10 BN RESUMED INDEPENDENT
FORMATION FROM 1918 JUNE AS ABOVE

CONFIDENTIAL

10th HIGHLAND LIGHT INFANTRY

WAR DIARY FOR JUNE 1918.

Army Form C. 2118.

WAR DIARY
or
INTELLIGENCE SUMMARY.
(Erase heading not required.)

Instructions regarding War Diaries and Intelligence Summaries are contained in F. S. Regs., Part II. and the Staff Manual respectively. Title pages will be prepared in manuscript.

Place	Date	Hour	Summary of Events and Information	Remarks and references to Appendices
ESQUELBECQ	1/6/18 –2/6/18		At ESQUELBECQ according notices to proceed to join 31st Division. Instruction classes were continued for the members of the training staff and all preparation for the move went on.	Mn
do.	3/6/18.		The Battalion Order presented at 9.30 am and marched to ARNEKE entraining there at 12.30 pm. MARQUISE was the next station about 6 pm. From MARQUISE the Battalion marched to RETY (CALAIS Sheet 13). Bn. HQ. established in house at road junction immediately killed to the Church. Notification was received that the training staff were to affiliated to South of the 311th Regt. A.E.F. for training purposes and was the Regiment arrived on the following day.	Mn
RETY	4/6/18		Active making the headquarters Company of the 311th Regiment arrived. inspecting Inspection, supper and lectures. Third number not 1 per centum was present to having them up to billets and attending them to the lecture rooms of a Company in the field. Saturday set for per preclusion etc.	Mn
do	5/6/18		In the forenoon the Headquarters Staff arrived from CALAIS and later the 1st Battalion of the Regiment. The Headquarters Staff are billeted to RETY and the 1st Battalion to an arrangement were made to begin instruction and repetition to the period, and programmes were submitted by the Specialist Officers.	Mn
do.	6/6/18		The day was spent by the 1st Battalion in clearing up and settling down to the ordinary routine of Gibbets. The 2nd Battalion of the Regiment arrived and was billeted in REBERTINGUE. One British Cay. Corporals are attached to each American Battalion. Ball is an	Mn

ESQUELBECQ

REBERTINGUE.
D. D. & L., London, E.C.

Army Form C. 2118.

WAR DIARY
or
INTELLIGENCE SUMMARY.
(Erase heading not required.)

Instructions regarding War Diaries and Intelligence Summaries are contained in F.S. Regs., Part II. and the Staff Manual respectively. Title pages will be prepared in manuscript.

Place	Date	Hour	Summary of Events and Information	Remarks and references to Appendices
RETY	7/6/18		Showery. Capacity space. The day in cleaning up and settling in billets. In the host Battalion the 2nd Battalion came and the three Battalions were ready. The remainder of the Battalion mess and quarters.	Nm.
Do.	8/6/18		Battalion Classes Commenced to the 2nd Battalion. Regimental Classes commenced at RETY in Rue Sue Gas.	Nm.
Do.	9/6/18		Sunday. Church Parade was held. No training was done.	Nm.
Do.	10/6/18 – 11/6/18		Training Continues at RETY. On 10/6/18 Regimental Classes to training and immediately commenced at Headquarters to training. Staff to move out to the 3rd L.I. Regt. to new training area at BRUNEMBERT.	Nm.
Do.	12/6/18		The Battalion marched out of RETY at 9.30 a.m. en route to BRUNEMBERT. Bn HQ was attached to the Schoolhouse. The remainder of the Bn. was spread in settling down in billets, remounting the new training area and making arrangements for the reception of Reynolds and half other areas. During the morning of the Reynolds School Shares to taken over by the 14th Regt. L.I. and also the School House is located at TURQUES, the 10/11th Regt. L.I. being billeted separately for the training of the Artillery Regt. and the Bn. instructors are posted and distributed amongst the centres of Battalion Classes. Arrangements have been made for the Regimental schools.	Nm.
BRUNEMBERT	13/6/18			Nm.

Army Form C. 2118.

WAR DIARY
or
INTELLIGENCE SUMMARY.
(Erase heading not required.)

Instructions regarding War Diaries and Intelligence Summaries are contained in F.S. Regs., Part II. and the Staff Manual respectively. Title pages will be prepared in manuscript.

Place	Date	Hour	Summary of Events and Information	Remarks and references to Appendices
BRUNEMBERT	14/6/18 -15/6/18		Training continued. On 15/6/18 orders were received that 10/11 Hvy. L.I. would hold itself in readiness to proceed to England and be reconstituted.	
do.	16/6/18		Final orders received and preparations made. At 5 pm the Battalion entrained. Staff marches out of BRUNEMBERT and proceeded to DESVRES when it entrained for BOULOGNE. Night spent in OSTROHOVE REST CAMP. When marched to proceed to ENGLAND on the following day with 14th Division.	
BOULOGNE	17/6/18		Embarked for FOLKESTONE about 10 a.m. and proceeded on arrival to BROOKWOOD SURREY. Accommodated in COWSHOTT No 2. Camp.	
BROOKWOOD	18/6/18 -21/6/18		At COWSHOTT CAMP. Personnel of 22nd Hvy. L.I. arriving daily for DEAL. Battalion being 10th Hvy. L.I. book of equipped and organising commenced. On 21/6/18 the Battalion moved from COWSHOTT CAMP to BULLSWATER No 1. Camp PIRBRIGHT.	
PIRBRIGHT	22/6/18 -30/6/18		Work of organisation and equipment continued. Entries with & amusement annual of Training. Musketry on BISLEY Ranges was carried out daily, and sweat note marches to many heads. War kits. Training in every branch hindered by the fact that kit store of Class III had large been over due to improvements, but these had not the later of nationality bamboo the aspects of all made preventing arrivals was sent to the additionally Blackdown Barracks, Frimley had reported and taken Cadre. Numerous	

WAR DIARY
or
INTELLIGENCE SUMMARY.

(Erase heading not required.)

Army Form C. 2118.

Place	Date	Hour	Summary of Events and Information	Remarks and references to Appendices
			Inspection has been made that two practically improves in training has been cut. Strength has about 630 all ranks fit. Training when received for to prepare to proceed in French Division on 4/7/18.	

P.M. Scoffin
Lt. Col.
Comdg. 10th Hants L.I.

CONFIDENTIAL

10th HIGH. L. I.

WAR DIARY

for

July 1918.

28031 W3125/M2250 1000m 6/17 M.R.Co.,Ltd. (1367) Forms W3091.   Army Form W. 3091.

Cover for Documents.

~~PENDING.~~

Natures of Enclosures.

Notes, or Letters written.

Army Form C. 2118.

WAR DIARY
or
INTELLIGENCE SUMMARY.
(Erase heading not required.)

Instructions regarding War Diaries and Intelligence Summaries are contained in F. S. Regs., Part II. and the Staff Manual respectively. Title pages will be prepared in manuscript.

Place	Date	Hour	Summary of Events and Information	Remarks and references to Appendices
BULLSWATER CAMP PIRBRIGHT	1/7/18	12 noon / 3 pm	Battalion inspected in full marching order by B.G.C. 43rd Inf. Bde. Transport inspected in full marching order at 3 pm. Draft of about 100 O.R. received.	am
"	2/7/18		Training Continued. D. Coy fired 2 application and 1 rapid practice on BISLEY ranges. The C.O. inspected no. of half: received yesterday. Short Battalion Route March in afternoon	pm
"	3/7/18	9 pm	Training Continued in Camp. Atny spent in preparing for move tomorrow. Transport entrained for SOUTHAMPTON.	pm
"	4/7/18	11.45 pm / 12.15 am (5/7/18)	Final preparations for move carried out. The Battalion entrained at BROOKWOOD STATION at 11.45 pm and 12.15 am (5/7/18) for FOLKESTONE.	pm
FOLKESTONE	5/7/18	1.30 pm / 11 am	At No 3 Rest Camp. Battalion sailed at 1.30pm for BOULOGNE and proceeded on arrival to OSTROHOVE Rest Camp where remains to proceed by train from BOULOGNE to MARQUISE about 11 am the following morning.	pm
BOULOGNE	6/7/18	11.30 am	Battalion entrained at 11.30 am at BOULOGNE Station and proceeded to MARQUISE. Marched from MARQUISE to Billet in MESNIL on the BOURIN area (CALAIS Sheet 13 1/100000).	am

Army Form C. 2118.

WAR DIARY
or
INTELLIGENCE SUMMARY.
(Erase heading not required.)

Instructions regarding War Diaries and Intelligence Summaries are contained in F.S. Regs., Part II. and the Staff Manual respectively. Title pages will be prepared in manuscript.

Place	Date	Hour	Summary of Events and Information	Remarks and references to Appendices
MESNIL	7/7/18		Army available to clearing up of roads and equipment and to settling down to billets. Conference held at B.HQ at 2·30 pm. Arrangements made for training.	[initials]
"	8/7/18		Training Commenced. Training of L.S.G teams. Grouping and Application practices fired on COLEMBERT range.	[initials]
"	9/7/18		Coy Sports at MONT DES BOUCARDS training area. Bayonet drill, rifle exercises, specialist training etc. Section Comrs and Sect. Runners went recce on the training area.	[initials]
"	10/7/18		Training Continued. Battalion paraded at 8 am musketry on COLEMBERT range. Staff ride for C.O.s and specialists under B.G.C. Orders received for move to ALEMBON on following day.	[initials]
"	11/7/18	7·30 am	Battalion paraded and marched to ALEMBON. HQ and 2 Coys billeted in ALEMBON and 2 Coys in SANGHEN.	[initials]
ALEMBON	12/7/18		Battalion marched to Billets in TOURNEHEM via LISQUES and CLERQUES.	[initials]
TOURNEHEM	13/7/18		Battalion marched to billets in NORTLEULINGHEM.	[initials]

Army Form C. 2118.

WAR DIARY
or
INTELLIGENCE SUMMARY.
(Erase heading not required.)

Instructions regarding War Diaries and Intelligence Summaries are contained in F. S. Regs., Part II. and the Staff Manual respectively. Title pages will be prepared in manuscript.

Place	Date	Hour	Summary of Events and Information	Remarks and references to Appendices
NORTLEUVINGHEM	14/7/18		Sunday. Church Parade. Stay otherwise devoted to cleaning up.	An
"	15/7/18		Training Continued. 6:30am – 7:20am. Handling of Arms. 8:30am – 9:30am. Inspection of Companies by Coy Commanders followed by Company drill. Musketry on "A" Range from 1 pm.	An
"	16/7/18		Corps Attended Battle of Divisional Band. EPERLECQUES. Training continued. Bombing classes commenced.	An
"	17/7/18		Brigade inspected by the Army Commander 2nd Army at 2:15 pm on field immediately N. of NORDAUSQUES – MOULLE road and between NORTLEULINGHEM and BAYENGHEM. Band of 10/11 u Highl. L.I. beyond from Staff.	An
"	18/7/18		Training continued. Wiring and Bombing practice carried out.	An
"	19/7/18		Battalion paraded to strength to provide and commence front guard marching armed at "A" Kings. A Hairdress band was lent as the Evening to the Nederd Cabaret Bn HQ Mess	An
"	20/7/18		Training Continued. Coy drill. Open order work. Wireless digging and wiring.	An

A5834 Wt.W4973/M687 730,000 8/16 D. D. & L. Ltd. Forms/C.2118/13.

Army Form C. 2118.

WAR DIARY
or
INTELLIGENCE SUMMARY.
(Erase heading not required.)

Instructions regarding War Diaries and Intelligence Summaries are contained in F. S. Regs, Part II. and the Staff Manual respectively. Title pages will be prepared in manuscript.

Place	Date	Hour	Summary of Events and Information	Remarks and references to Appendices
NORTEULINGHEM	21/7/18		Sunday. Church Parade. At the afternoon a Reymondes Bouquet Competition was held. B.G.C. 43rd Bde. acted as judge.	Am
"	22/7/18		Battalion Lewis gun platoon Competition. Won by chief platoon L. Corporal. Brigade Competition. No 10 Platoon. C. Coy. (Lieut. T.C. Rice) won the platoon Demonstration carried out by 1st Army Musketry Camp on "B" Camp. Lecture at BAYENGHEM on Fire Tactics.	Am
"	23/7/18		General Musketry Course continues on "A" Range. Standing exposition of British etc by O.C. 42nd Field Ambulance. Lecture on "Intelligence" at BAYENGHEM.	Am
"	24/7/18		Training Continued. Brigade Transport Competition 3.15 p.m.	Am
"	25/7/18		General Musketry Course on "A" Range. "C" and "D" Coys. took long field practice on the ground of Competition. Lecture on Gas at NORTEULINGHEM.	Am
"	26/7/18		Training Continues. Different livings. Defence of a Post. Defence of a defensive locality.	Am

Army Form C. 2118.

WAR DIARY
or
INTELLIGENCE SUMMARY.
(Erase heading not required.)

Instructions regarding War Diaries and Intelligence Summaries are contained in F. S. Regs., Part II. and the Staff Manual respectively. Title pages will be prepared in manuscript.

Place	Date	Hour	Summary of Events and Information	Remarks and references to Appendices
NORTLEULINGHEM	27/7/18	6 am	Battalion marched to 'A' Camp to Continue musketry Course. Practice by men from troop and fireing to return to billets. Brigade platoon competition postponed because of weather until tomorrow	pm
	28/7/18		Sunday. Church Parade. Battn at EPERLECQUES. Men received for move to LA BRIARDE area for work under XV Corps. (Sheet 27 1/80000 V 6 c.)	pm
"	29/7/18	8.15 am	Beautime marches to Billets in TATINGHEM. Bn. HQ. Billet No 20.	pm
TATINGHEM	30/7/18	9.30 am	Battalion marched to billets at LES SIX RUES immediately W. of STAPLE (Sheet HAZEBROUCK 5A) arriving there 7 pm. Dinners are here taken in mess.	pm
STAPLE	31/7/18	11 am	Battalion marched to billets in STAPLE (Sheet 27 1/80000 W 1) Battalion HQ. establishes in farm W 1 a. 1.9. Battalion head 5 Commanders took over or on STAPLE — THIEUSHOEK defences. (Q 34 central — Q 35 central).	pm

M. Ingram
Lieut. Colonel
Comdg. 10th Kings L.I.

Secret.
Confidential.

10ᵀᴴ (S) Bₙ. High. L.I.

War Diary

for

August, 1918

28031 W3125/M2250 1000m 6/17 M.R.Co.,Ltd. (1367) Forms W3091. Army Form W. 3091.

Cover for Documents.

Nature of Enclosures.

PENDING.

10/11TH (S) BATTN.,
HIGHLAND
LIGHT INFANTRY.

No.
Date.

Notes, or Letters written.

WAR DIARY or INTELLIGENCE SUMMARY

Army Form C. 2118.

Place	Date	Hour	Summary of Events and Information	Remarks and references to Appendices
27/W1&1.9 CAESTRE	1-8-18 — 15.8.18.		During this period the battalion was employed in digging and wiring the THIESHOUK defences in Q.34 and 35 (Sheet 27 1/40000). Work commenced on August 1st and finished on Aug. 13th, and was carried out under the direction of the 224th Field Company R.E. Supervision by the C.R.E. LE PEUPLIER defences have been allotted by task and amounted to about seven hours work per day. Two companies were employed on the front and two companies on the support line of the THIESHOUK defences and each day about one company was engaged in wiring the line being dug. Meanwhile I was still posible to carry out a certain amount of training. Officers for Signallers and Lewis Gunners were sent to the various battalion schools there were several different platoon Commanders on 5th, 7th and 9th September a number of Officers attended Lieut General Morlan's lectures and demonstration at TERDIGHEM and each company Commander arranges a demonstration platoon of his own and the remainder of the company attended an informal parade of his support, to witness the demonstration.	

WAR DIARY or INTELLIGENCE SUMMARY.

Army Form C. 2118.

Place	Date	Hour	Summary of Events and Information	Remarks and references to Appendices
27/W1 A 1.9 near CAESTRE	1/8/18 – 15/8/18 (continued)		Sunday was devoted to holidays and inter-company and platoon football matches were organised. Aug 14th and 15th were devoted to cleaning up and preparing for the impending move. Various kit parades were held. Orders were received on Aug 14th to move to the DROGLANDT area on 16/8/18 and report to Brigade there.	Am.
do.	16/8/18.		The Battalion marched off at 6.30 am and proceeded to the road running W. of STEENVOORDE through P.24 and J.36 to DROGLANDT. Accommodation was found in towns and huts in T.6 and T.11. Bn. HQ. was established in a farm at K.2.C.0.6. Orders received to move on the following day to the PROVEN area. In the afternoon A Coy was despatched in advance to the 2nd Corps.	Am.
DROGLANDT	17/8/18		The Battalion left DROGLANDT at 7.30 am and marched by WATOU to PROVEN. where the Battalion was accommodated in PEKIN Camp. F.2.C. Orders received to move on 18/8/18 to ORILLIA CAMP VLAMERTINGHE.	Am.

WAR DIARY
or
INTELLIGENCE SUMMARY.
(Erase heading not required.)

Army Form C. 2118.

Place	Date	Hour	Summary of Events and Information	Remarks and references to Appendices
PROVEN	18/8/18		The Battalion entrained in his leave from PUGWASH station at 9.45 a.m. and proceeded to ORILLIA CAMP 28/H 2 a 6.5. Camp was reached by the 49th Division. There was a Presbyterian Church parade in Camp at 4 p.m. and a Cinema performance at 6 p.m.	8 p.m.
ORILLIA CAMP VLAMERTINGHE	19/8/18 – 23/8/18		The Battalion remained. On the nights 19th/20th & 43rd Bn. Bdes took over the Reserve Position of the 49th Divisional Front and the Battalion remained in Reserve at ORILLIA CAMP. Here the men were considered training Platoon and Company Kennans. Each Company was the time the devoted to platoon and Company training and some practice allotted a store map in the vicinity of the Camp and some practice was given to the movement on and tire of Lewis Gun teams. In addition Companies trained in the problem of attack and as far as possible the conditions to be met were simulated and new practices in particulars of the final line were Vimy Ridge and Messines area and in general Museum Memorial to area of the Suffolk Trenches and in general was made between the 12th Suffolk Regt. then in the right 23rd/24th	8 p.m.

WAR DIARY
or
INTELLIGENCE SUMMARY.
(Erase heading not required.)

Army Form C. 2118.

Place	Date	Hour	Summary of Events and Information	Remarks and references to Appendices
BOESTAY CASTLE VLAMERTINGHE H.11.6.8.3			At 8.30 pm 23/8/18 the Battalion left ORILLIA CAMP and proceeded to relieve the 12th Suffolk Regt in the Support position, Relief was completed about 11pm and was carried out without much difficulty in spite of some gas shelling in the vicinity of SHRAPNEL CROSSING H.11.6. O.O. One Company occupied the DOLL'S HOUSE area with 3 platoons having Headers extending from about I.14.a.2.9. to I.20.a.0.9. but no platoon to House Shelter. I.14.a.2.9. to I.20.a.0.9. but no platoon to House Shelter. Company manned the CANAL DEFENCES in I.13.c. Two Companies occupied shelters and dug outs in H.11 and H.12.	
	24/8/18 – 27/8/18		The period in Support was very quiet apart from occasional hostile shelling of Batteries in the vicinity of Bn. HQ and the rear Companies. Working parties were provided for the 208th Field Co. R.E. No training was possible because of the impossibility of movement by platoon of any size during the hours of daylight. Officers reconnoitred the front trench line with a view to relieving the 12th Suffolk Regt - on the night 27th/28th.	

Am.

WAR DIARY or INTELLIGENCE SUMMARY

Army Form C. 2118.

Place	Date	Hour	Summary of Events and Information	Remarks and references to Appendices
YPRES I.14.b.1.9 – I.11.b.1.8	28/8/18 – 31/8/18		On the night 27th/28th Aug the Battalion was relieved in the Stopper area by the 20th Middlesex Regt. Relief was complete at 11.15 p.m. On relief the Battalion proceeded to relieve the 12th Suffolk Regt in the line Battalion area. The Battalion front extended from I.16.a.6.4. to I.21.c.7.3. The front line was taken over by A Coy on the right, B Coy in the Centre and D Coy on the left. C Coy Coln took shelter in the YPRES DEFENCE LINE immediately east of the Ramparts. Relief was complete at 12.50 am. 28/8/18 The night was kept quiet and patrols with one Lewis gun team being laid on by the enemy. The Battalion who lay on the left were the 5th A.I.F. Inft on our right were the 120th American Regt. On the night 28/8/29th the 33rd London Regiment (B.B.) relieved the 5th A.I.F. Highlanders. 29.8.18 The night was again quiet. Listening patrols though fired on at various points did not encounter the enemy in strength. During the day enemy artillery activity increased, this embankment at western end of ZILLEBEKE LAKE being shelled with H.2 and 5.9. During the night 29th/30th Aug an inter-company relief was carried out, C Coy relieving D Coy on the left Coys any front	

Army Form C. 2118.

WAR DIARY
or
INTELLIGENCE SUMMARY.
(Erase heading not required.)

Place	Date	Hour	Summary of Events and Information	Remarks and references to Appendices
YPRES T.14.b.9	28/8/18 30/8/18		30:8:18 All day the areas of the western embankment of ZILLEBEKE LAKE was subjected to heavy fire which rose to extreme violency from 7 to 8 p.m. In view of the damage caused to A Coy's H.Q. at 11.S.d 00.15, Coy H.Q. was moved to I.21.b.15.45. For about from 7 p.m. to 8 p.m. A Coy's posts at I.21.b.1.6 & I.21.b.15.95 Nylon kopje half were withdrawn but were remounted at 8.15 p.m. AKJ	
	31/8/18		31:8:18 At 5.15 a.m. for 5 minutes a short 77 mm barrage was put down round A Coy's posts at I.21.b.2.8 & I.21.b.45.15. When the barrage lifted a party of about 20 enemy were seen approaching from I.22.C.0.9. They were held up by rifle & L.G. fire. A few minutes later a party of about 8 enemy attempted to advance along the Southern bank of the lake. On rifle fire being directed upon them, they withdrew. The larger party also withdrew. At 9.35 a.m. a message was received from 43rd Bde that enemy was reported to have evacuated KEMMEL & might possibly go back on the front of the 16th Bn(?). & ordering one platoon to be ready to go out on daylight patrol on receipt of further orders from Bde. "E" Coy was ordered to have a platoon ready for this purpose. AKJ	

WAR DIARY
or
INTELLIGENCE SUMMARY.
(Erase heading not required.)

Place	Date	Hour	Summary of Events and Information	Remarks and references to Appendices
YPRES	28/8/18 31/8/18		At 11.30 am an order was received from Bde to send out officers patrol at 12 noon to line ZILLEBEKE - LEINSTER FARM - CAMBRIDGE ROAD to ascertain whether the area west of that line was clear of enemy & secondly what points on that line were still held by the enemy. If the area was clear of the enemy the patrol was not to withdraw till further orders were received from Bde. At 2pm. No 9 Platoon under Lt. A. MACKAY left to carry out reconnaissance as ordered. The platoon reached a position about I.16.b.30.35 where fire was opened on them by two rifles. They remained there for some time when a heavy fire was opened on them from all sides. Eight men only returned later. a party went out in search of wounded but found no one. At 5.35pm. In accordance with instructions from Bde. a platoon of A Coy under 2/Lt. J.A.ROSS moved forward to occupy MANOR FARM if possible. The platoon reached a position about I.22.c.05.70 apparently	

WH.

Army Form C. 2118.

WAR DIARY
or
INTELLIGENCE SUMMARY.
(Erase heading not required.)

Instructions regarding War Diaries and Intelligence Summaries are contained in F. S. Regs., Part II. and the Staff Manual respectively. Title pages will be prepared in manuscript.

Place	Date	Hour	Summary of Events and Information	Remarks and references to Appendices
YPRES	28/8/18 3/1/9/18		Apparently gained touch with patrols of the 120th (American) Regiment on the right but from the left they encountered strong rifle & M.G. fire. Two sections from another platoon were sent out to cover the exposed flank. It was soon apparent however that the enemy were present in strength. Along the southern side of ZILLEBEKE LAKE & runners were sent out with instructions for the platoon & sections to withdraw gradually. They reached our lines about 8·45 p.m. During the operation 2/Lt ROSS & one L.G. team were separated from their platoon. 2/Lt ROSS was severely wounded and the L.G. knocked out & had to be abandoned. The remainder of the party were casualties or badly shaken & were unable to bring 2/Lt ROSS in the loop. On learning this an officer & 4 O.R. went out to bring in Lt ROSS but were unable to find him.	J.R.Y. M. Ingham Lieut Col Com'd'g 13 Ryls L.I.

A5834 Wt. W4973/M687 750,000 8/16 D. D. & L. Ltd. Forms/C.2118/13.

Army Form C. 2118.

WAR DIARY
or
INTELLIGENCE SUMMARY.
(Erase heading not required.)

Place	Date	Hour	Summary of Events and Information	Remarks and references to Appendices
			Casualties for period 28th to 31st August 1918 (inclusive)	
			Officers Other Ranks	
			Killed — 1	
			Wounded — 15 (1 at duty)	
			Wounded missing 1 4	
			Missing 1 15	
			N.Y.D.N. cases — 4	
			Total 2 39	
				M Benjamin Lieut Col
				Comdg 10th High. L.I.

Instructions regarding War Diaries and Intelligence Summaries are contained in F. S. Regs., Part II. and the Staff Manual respectively. Title pages will be prepared in manuscript.

CONFIDENTIAL

WAR DIARY

OF

10th HIGH. L. I.

FOR

SEPTEMBER 1918

28031 W3125/M2250 1000m 6/17 M.R.Co.,Ltd. (1367) Forms W3091.   Army Form W. 3091.

Cover for Documents.

TRAINING

Natures of Enclosures.

Notes, or Letters written.

Army Form C. 2118.

WAR DIARY
or
INTELLIGENCE SUMMARY.
(Erase heading not required.)

Instructions regarding War Diaries and Intelligence Summaries are contained in F. S. Regs., Part II. and the Staff Manual respectively. Title pages will be prepared in manuscript.

Place	Date	Hour	Summary of Events and Information	Remarks and references to Appendices
Front Line	1/9/18		A very quiet day with nothing to report. On the night of Sept 1st/2nd the Battalion was relieved by the 20th Middlesex Regt. and on relief proceeded to the Bde. Reserve Position in ORILLIA CAMP. near VLAMERTINGHE 28/H 2 & 6.7.	AM
YPRES Sector Bn. HQ. I.16.b.1.9.				
VLAMERTINGHE	2/9/18 - 6/9/18		In Bde. Reserve in ORILLIA CAMP. The first day was devoted to cleaning up of men and equipment. One battery at SIEGE BATHS B 20 d.9.1. Training began on the following morning. Musketry drill and musketry parades were carried out and during the period men were given practice in patrolling. As men were available, Lewis gun and Rifle grenade, wiring and gas helmet improvement, was started. Anti-aircraft and rifle exercises were also practised. On the night of Sept 6th/7th the Battalion proceeded to the Support Area and relieved the 12th Suffolk Regt. (Bn. HQ. BOBSTAY CASTLE H.11.b.8.3.)	AM
Bde. Support Area Bn. HQ BOBSTAY CASTLE	7/9/18 -11/9/18		On Sept 7th Lt. Col. A.H. Seaguim left for CO's Course at 2nd Army School. WISQUES and Command of the Battalion was taken over by Major J. JOHNSTON. During the period working parties were found to work on Support line under R.E. supervision. On the night Sept. 11th/12th the Battalion was relieved by the 20th Middlesex Regt.	AM

Army Form C. 2118.

WAR DIARY (continued)
or
INTELLIGENCE SUMMARY.
(Erase heading not required.)

Instructions regarding War Diaries and Intelligence Summaries are contained in F.S. Regs., Part II. and the Staff Manual respectively. Title pages will be prepared in manuscript.

Place	Date	Hour	Summary of Events and Information	Remarks and references to Appendices
Front Line YPRES Sector Bn. H.Q. I.14.b.1.9.	12/9/18 –14/9/18.		(Relief complete 10 pm) and on relief proceeded to front line arriving 12th Supports Rest. (Relief complete 12.56 am). In the front position B. Coy night front Company and Supply front Coy. A Coy was to provide 2 platoons for the test of the Ramparts. C Coy had 2 platoons in Support to B Coy and 2 platoons in the MAGAZINE YPRES front line under R.E. On the night of the battalion front was the 1/1st Yorkshire Dragoons and on its left the 16th Manchester Regt. 42nd Inf Bde. During this period in the line nothing of interest whatever took place and the line was infantry taken up but a series of shell reliefs were necessary by the reorganisation of the front. On the night Sept. 12th/13th the two platoons of C. Coy in support to B Coy were known to A Coy turned to the Reserve line. On the night Sept 13th/14th half of the night company front (B. Coy) was taken over by the Yorkshire Dragoons. Information received that the battalion would be relieved on the following nights. Sept. 14th/15th B. Coy were relieved by A Coy of 1/1st Yorkshire Dragoons On the night Sept. 14th/15th B. Coy were relieved by a Company of 5th Coy was relieved by D Coy 29th D.L.I. A Coy was relieved by the 33rd London Regt. R.B. (Relief complete 11 pm). The Battalion proceeded by train from	9 am.

A 5834 Wt. W 4973/M687 750,000 8/16 D.D. & L. Ltd. Forms/C.2118/13.

WAR DIARY (Anthonies) or INTELLIGENCE SUMMARY.

Army Form C. 2118.

Place	Date	Hour	Summary of Events and Information	Remarks and references to Appendices
SCHOOLS CAMP ST. JAN TER BIEZEN.	16/9/18 – 20/9/18.		GUDERICH SIDING I.C.I.8 to ST JAN TER BIEZEN School Accommodation hen provided in SCHOOLS CAMP 27/L3C5.3. The period at SCHOOLS CAMP was devoted to platoon and Company training. Each day munition parades were available for use by Companies and 2 hours each of steadying harness to musketry were carried out. On September 18th and 19th an attack practise on a similar Company front, the exercises were held by daylight over ground South of the camp. Companies lined up on tapes and advanced in waves of sections. Smoke bombs were used to represent our barrage and on the second day a correct place Corporation and the Arts were employed by Personal Officer. On Sept 19th instructions were received that the battalion would relieve a battalion of the 42nd Inf. Bde. in the night 20th/21st Sept. to the front line astride the YPRES – COMINES CANAL at 28/I326 and d. The 20th was spent in preparations for the move and at 7pm the battalion left in buses for the forward area. Relief of the 6th Wilts Regt. by C Coy front, D Coy Support to the forward area. A Coy left front, C Coy Regt front, B Coy Support in CH. SEGARD area and B Coy in Reserve in the region of CAFE FARM.	Apx. Apx.

WAR DIARY (continued)
or
INTELLIGENCE SUMMARY.

Army Form C. 2118.

Place	Date	Hour	Summary of Events and Information	Remarks and references to Appendices
Front Line. Bn. HQ. A.24.c.5.3. (Sheet 28)	21/9/18 — 25/9/18.		A quiet period devoted principally to preparing the area for forthcoming operations. Work on existing trench tramline area carried out. Each front Company sent out daylight and dusk patrols from the out-post line to the region of MIDDLESEX ROAD. No sitting patrols of note observed. On 25/9/18 an old veteran of the 40th Saxon Div. lost his way and gave himself up to one of our posts and from him considerable information was obtained not regard to the enemy's movements and intentions. That night a patrol of 1/OO.O.R. who passed from the Sappers Company for the construction of a mud track. On the trek this bright patrol was supplied for carrying up ammunition and water for the formation of forward dumps at the front Company headquarters. The Battalion was relieved by 2 Coys of the 12th Suffolk Regt. and 2 Coys of the 20th Middlesex Regt. under O.C. 12th Suffolk Regt. on the night of Sept. 25/26th (Relief Complete 2.20 am) and on relief proceeded to huts to WINNEZEELE area Accommodation being found in an annexe a farm close to hill N.W. of STEENVOORDE on the STEENVOORDE - DROGLANDT Road.	MM
STEENVOORDE	26/9/18.		Main Remnant Arrived in huts at 26/27th to DOMINION CAMP 28/G.24.a. then and at 6.20pm the Battalion The day was spent in resting entrained at STEENVOORDE JUNCTION and proceeded by light railway to DOMINION CAMP.	MM

A.5834 Wt.W4973/M687 750,000 8/16 D.D.&L. Ltd. Forms/C.2118/13.

WAR DIARY (Continued)
or
INTELLIGENCE SUMMARY

Army Form C. 2118.

Place	Date	Hour	Summary of Events and Information	Remarks and references to Appendices
DOMINION CAMP G 24 a (Sheet 28)	27/9/18		Final instructions received for forthcoming operations. The next orders for the attack are 28/9/18 and the two objectives allotted to the 47th Div. Batt. were as follows:-	
			1st Objective O.3.c.25.30. The BLUFF (inclusive) thence along YPRES-COMINES CANAL to O.5.a.	
			2nd Objective The line WHITE CHATEAU — TRIANGULAR BLUFF.	
			Therefore the operation this entailed was that the 12th Suffolk Regt. and the 20th Middlesex Regt. were the first objective Batts. to reach St. Ita to the KRUINSTRAATHOEK forward up at Zero hour with 2 Coys. each and 2 Coys. east of the MIDDLESEX ROAD area and HORNSBY ROAD, and at Zero to advance to the MIDDLESEX ROAD area and after supplied by necessary stores ammunition.	
			The 27th Sept. was spent in preparing for the move forward and in drawing extra ammunition bombs, took the extra carried on the men.	
			About 6.30 p.m. the battalion headed nw- of DOMINION CAMP and proceeded by H 13 central H 14 6 and DEN GROENEN JAGER CAB.T to the CAFE FARM area as to H 23 C and at where a halt of a few hours was made pending the moving up into position of the troops to the line.	
			At 12 midnight 27th/28th Sept the battalion move forward and at Zero hour (5:30 am 28/9/18) left Dugout as below.	

WAR DIARY (continued)
or
INTELLIGENCE SUMMARY

Army Form C. 2118.

Place	Date	Hour	Summary of Events and Information	Remarks and references to Appendices
In Action	28/9/18 – 29/9/18		Bn. HQ. H 2L c 5.3. A and C Coys. CHATEAU SEGARD area H 30 b. and d. B and D Coys. VIMY area I 25 c and d. At Zero hour the battalion moved forward. Bn. H.Q. to LANKHOF CHATEAU I 32.a 90.96. Companies to the MIDDLESEX ROAD area. D Coy left front, B Coy right front, A Coy left support, C Coy right support. The men were completed without great difficulty in spite of the heavy barrage which dropped shortly after Zero about the line of the YPRES – WYTSCHAETE ROAD. An ambulance to shout – our own. Both Assaulting forces (seen by the Brigade) fulfilled the necessity of calling for every help from the battalion. At 11.15 am B Coy moved up to fill a gap in the line of the front attacking troops between the 20th Middlesex Regt. and the 42nd Inf. Bde. and C Coy moved forward to SPOIL BANK. At 5.15 pm to relieve all Coys South of the CANAL and so more hastily available for but in the heart of any counter attack developing. A Coy moved to area I 32 d 6.3. – I 32 d 90.35. D Coy between I 32 d 90.35. – I 33 c 40.35. A Coy 33rd London Regt. we attached to Lt. I 32.a 90.35. – I 33 c 40.35. B Coy del moved to support 20th Middlesex Regt. and both Hardecourt to replace B Coys del moved to I 32.a 20.35. – I 32 c 60.92.	

Army Form C. 2118.

WAR DIARY (continued)
or
INTELLIGENCE SUMMARY.
(Erase heading not required.)

Place	Date	Hour	Summary of Events and Information	Remarks and references to Appendices
PIONEER CAMP H 21 6.7.	30/9/18		Water and SAA were carried forward to the front battalions, and the supply passed through C. Coy who also provided 2 scouts as Runner Company. At 9.45 20th Middlesex Regt. and A Coy London Regt. moved to the SPOIL BANK to relieve C Coy. Meanwhile word to front had been developing and the 34th Division on our right had advanced down and taken up both the 41st Division centre and reserve line the 1st Division was withdrawn at Lock S. W. 5 pm. Orders were received from the Brigade. By 10pm Bn. HQ and 3 Coys had been recommended at H 21.6 to disgorge and shelter in the vicinity of PIONEER CAMP. B Coy which had been in the front line with the 20th Middlesex Regt. arrived about midnight. Total casualties during operations: Lieut. S. DONALDSON A Coy killed, 9 OR wounded. An Australian Field Ambulance is in PIONEER area. Stay awaits to relieving the Europeans. An M. Scotson Lt. Colonel. Comdg. 10th Regt. L.I.

10TH H.L.I

WAR DIARY

OCTOBER 1918

35807. W16879/M1879 500,000 3/17 R.T. (1074) Forms/W3091/3 — Army Form W.3091.

Cover for Documents.

BM/234

Nature of Enclosures.

C.O.

10/11TH (S) BATTN.,
HIGHLAND
LIGHT INFANTRY.

No.
Date.

Notes, or Letters written.

WAR DIARY
or
INTELLIGENCE SUMMARY.
(Erase heading not required.)

Army Form C. 2118.

Place	Date	Hour	Summary of Events and Information	Remarks and references to Appendices
PIONEER CAMP	1:10:18		The Battalion continued to rest	MJ
POTIJZE	2:10:18		The Battalion was placed at the disposal of the 2nd Corps for work on roads under C.E. and moved by march route to camping ground near POTIJZE. Tents were pitched after the camp site had been cleared and levelled. As there were insufficient tents to accommodate the whole Battalion, corrugated iron "wood" huts were salved and shelters erected for the remainder.	MJ
	3:10:18		Road-making work was carried out on MENIN ROAD at INVERNESS COPSE & HOOGE CRATER. Four companies were so employed	MJ
	4:10:18		do	MJ
	5:10:18 to 11:10:18		Similar work on road west of ZONNEBE	MJ

Army Form C. 2118.

WAR DIARY
or
INTELLIGENCE SUMMARY.
(Erase heading not required.)

Instructions regarding War Diaries and Intelligence Summaries are contained in F. S. Regs., Part II. and the Staff Manual respectively. Title pages will be prepared in manuscript.

Place	Date	Hour	Summary of Events and Information	Remarks and references to Appendices
WULVERGHEM AREA & MESSINES	12/10/18		The Battalion entrained at 09.45 at HELLFIRE CORNER I10.c.9.2 and proceeded by rail to WULVERGHEM where it bivouacked until dusk when it moved to bivouac shelters in 28/O.33.a.4. near MESSINES. The Brigade then became Brigade in support, the 41st Brigade being in the line near COMINES, from 28/V.8.c.5.0. My to P.3.b.a.5.6.	
	13.10.18 14.10.18		Battalion remained in position under 30 minutes notice to move. Reconnaissances of lines were carried out by all officers.	
WERVICQ	15.10.18 16.10.18		The 43rd Brigade received orders to relieve the 21st Brigade in WERVICQ. The Batt. moved by march route at 09.30 to relieve the 1st Cheshire Regiment. Owing the darkness & the fact that two companies had to cross the River LYS on a bridge that had been practically destroyed the relief was not complete till 06.15. The line taken up by the two front companies B & D ran through W.2.a and R and W.3.a.a.b.	

WAR DIARY
or
INTELLIGENCE SUMMARY.
(Erase heading not required.)

Army Form C. 2118.

Place	Date	Hour	Summary of Events and Information	Remarks and references to Appendices
WERVICQ	16:10:18		Immediately after relief B. Coys pushed forward on to high ground in W 2 c and W 3 c. No enemy was encountered but no instance. Troops were observed in small numbers and auxiliary M.G. fire was met with. The 12th Suffolk Regt. then took over the line and B Coys. moved into WHITE CHATEAU Area in support of them. During the afternoon the enemy shelled WERVICQ SUD, PAULBUCQ and the neighbouring country for four hours with heavy guns.	M.Y.
WERVICQ & RONCQ	17:10:18		At 15.30 orders were received from Brigade to advance to a line along the road from X 25 central to RONCQ, the 12th Suffolk Regt. on the Right, the 10th R.F. on the left with the 20th Mdsex in support. At 15.35 the Battalion moved, C. Coys. Companies in front & A+B Companies in support. The Battalion proceeded by march route, protected by a screen of scouts and occupied the line without opposition by 18.30, Batt. H.Q. at SINGLET FARM, 28/W 12 d 4.7. Casualties 2 O.R. Wounded	M.Y.

WAR DIARY
or
INTELLIGENCE SUMMARY.
(Erase heading not required.)

Army Form C. 2118.

Place	Date	Hour	Summary of Events and Information	Remarks and references to Appendices
RONCQ to MOUSCRON	18/10/18		In accordance with orders the Battalion moved at 10.00 continuing the advance towards MOUSCRON. On approaching NEUVILLE FERRAIN about 12.30, information was received that there were probable M.G. posts between that village and MOUSCRON. Accordingly C. Company advanced to occupy road from BLANC PIGNON S14b.6.3 to CHEMIN CROISÉ in S9c.6.4 M.G. Coy advanced across country to an objective having as its boundaries, road junction BLANC PIGNON, and S15c.6.0. No opposition being met with B.H.Q. Companies moved on to occupy the Eastern outskirts of MOUSCRON, B. Coy on the left reaching the railway line from PETIT CORNIL to S17a.9.8 about 17.00 after heavy resistance. D. Coy. was held up but attacked at 18.00 and after considerable resistance reached a line from S17a.6.8 to S.29 central at 23.00, gaining touch with B. Coy. on the left and the 20th Middlesex on the right. B. Coy. captured two prisoners of the 38th Regt. The advance was carried out in co-operation with D. Coy. 14th M.G. Batt.	

WAR DIARY
or
INTELLIGENCE SUMMARY.
(Erase heading not required.)

Army Form C. 2118.

Place	Date	Hour	Summary of Events and Information	Remarks and references to Appendices
MOUSCRON	18/10/18		Patrols were pushed out during the night to a distance of 2000 yards but no enemy was encountered. During the afternoon MOUSCRON Square & the outskirts of the town were heavily shelled. The Battalion were the first troops to enter the town on the heels of the enemy. Casualties 6 O.R. wounded. The Battalion was in Brigade Support on this day and at 16.30 moved to HERSEAUX where the night was spent in billets.	
HERSEAUX	19/10/18		The Battalion remained in Brigade Support. On this day the Brigade advanced to the line of the SCHELDT River. "A" Coy was detached & arrived at ST. LEGER at 15.16 where they formed a defensive flank on the right of the Brigade. At 17.00 the Brigade having gained touch with the 31st Divn. on the right A. Coy. withdrew and spent the night at ST. LEGER. The remainder of the Battalion spent the night in TRIEU.	
TRIEU	20/10/18			

Army Form C. 2118.

WAR DIARY
or
INTELLIGENCE SUMMARY.
(Erase heading not required.)

Instructions regarding War Diaries and Intelligence Summaries are contained in F. S. Regs., Part II. and the Staff Manual respectively. Title pages will be prepared in manuscript.

Place	Date	Hour	Summary of Events and Information	Remarks and references to Appendices
QUEVAUCAMP	21/10/18		The Brigade was relieved by 42nd Brigade and the Battalion withdrew to billets in QUEVAUCAMP at 17.00	904
	22/10/18 to 31/10/18		The Battalion rested in billets in QUEVAUCAMP and refitted. Training was resumed, special attention being paid to Open Warfare. On 24th Oct. Lt Col. A.H. SEAGRIM proceeded to ENGLAND on leave and MAJOR JAMES JOHNSTON assumed Command	904 904 904

James Johnston Major
Cmdg 10 b.R.F.

War Diary
10th Highland L.I.
November 1918

Army Form C. 2118.

WAR DIARY
or
INTELLIGENCE SUMMARY.
(Erase heading not required.)

Place	Date	Hour	Summary of Events and Information	Remarks and references to Appendices
QUEVAUCAMP	1/11/18		The Battalion rested in billets. Training was carried on, special stress being laid on practising open fighting.	
	7/11/18			
HELCHIN	8/11/18		This Battalion relieved the 2nd D.L.I. near HELCHIN in the left sub-sector of the Brigade front, the 12th Suffolk Regt. being on the right. There were no trenches, except on the line being an outpost line owing to a traffic block which delayed the Lewis Gun limbers and to the difficulty of crossing the SCHELDT to some of the posts, relief was not complete till 05.00 on the 9th.	
	9/11/18		Owing the extraordinary quietness during the relief, it was considered probable that the enemy had withdrawn. Accordingly C. Coy was ordered to send out patrols to obtain enemy posts. The enemy having retired, our patrols occupied the enemy posts. C. Coy was then ordered forward to take up a position on the GUERMIGNIES - LANNOY ROAD from 37/C5d7.6 to C6b2.6. This move was completed about 06.15. A. Coy was then moved forward to a position on the same road from C11a5.3 to	

WAR DIARY
or
INTELLIGENCE SUMMARY

Army Form C. 2118.

Place	Date	Hour	Summary of Events and Information	Remarks and references to Appendices
	10/11/18		C.5d.7.6. Both Coys. then pushed out patrols to line of road from D.1.c.3.3. to C.7.b.8.8. No opposition was met. At 07.45 Both Coys. advanced on to this line. At the same time D & B Coys. crossed the SCHELDT. The move was complete by 09.30. At 11.15 A Coy. had reached railway line through C.18.6 & D.13.a. At 11.59 Batt. Headquarters were established at FME DE NAVERIE. The advance continued but at 17.05 orders were received from Brigade to concentrate in the neighbourhood of FME DE NAVERIE D.3.c.3.8. as the 29th & 40th Divisions had pinched us out. No enemy was encountered. There were no casualties. M.H.	
FME DE NAVERIE	11/11/18		The Battalion was employed filling up mine craters on the roads in the immediate neighbourhood. On the 11th news was received of the signing of the Armistice & the cessation of hostilities. Lt.Col. SEAGRIM resumed command on the 11th. M.H.	

Army Form C. 2118.

WAR DIARY
or
INTELLIGENCE SUMMARY.
(Erase heading not required.)

Instructions regarding War Diaries and Intelligence Summaries are contained in F. S. Regs., Part II. and the Staff Manual respectively. Title pages will be prepared in manuscript.

Place	Date	Hour	Summary of Events and Information	Remarks and references to Appendices
ST LEGER	13/11/18		The Battalion moved by march route to ST. LEGER where two days were spent checking up.	
	14/11/18			
TOURCOING	15/11/18		The Battalion moved by march route to billets in TOURCOING where it settled down to barrack conditions. Palliasses & iron bed Cows forms Stables being supplied. Two officers and 50 o.r.o represented the Battalion at a special Thanksgiving Service at ROUBAIX on the 17th. On the 25th the Brigade was inspected by the Corps Commander. While certain parades still continued, an Education Scheme was started within the Battalion & parties were formed & attended lectures arranged by the Corps.	
	30/11/18			

Lt Colonel
Cmdg 10th Bn C.M.R.
2/4/19

SECRET Vol 43

32-L
5 sheets

10th HIGH. L.I.

WAR DIARY FOR DECEMBER 1918

WAR DIARY
INTELLIGENCE SUMMARY. MM.

Army Form C. 2118.

Place	Date	Hour	Summary of Events and Information	Remarks and references to Appendices
TOURCOING	1st to 7th Dec. 1918		Training. Half-hour parades for NCOs are held daily under the Adjutant in the Yard of the Douane Station (cnr. of RUE WINOC CHOCQUEEL). Companies carried out 1 hour's steady drill daily on Company parade grounds. On Friday Dec. 6th a rehearsal parade was held in MOUVEAUX in view of having inspection of the Division by the Army Commander. Saturday Dec 7th is devoted to the Scrubbing of Webbing and the inspection of kits. Education. Classes are held in French and Shorthand, also a class for Illiterates. Two lectures were attended, one on "Exploration" and the other on "Industrial Peace". A debate on the subject of "Back to the land" was carried out in the Bn. Recreation Room. The Divisional Boxing Contest took place during the week. On Friday 6th a battalion concert was held in the French Priests' School, RUE DE LA MALCENSE. Among the best companies received front and Influenza inoculation. On Dec 3rd a party of about 40 from the battalion took part in the Divisional Tattoo in ROUBAIX.	MM.

Army Form C. 2118.

WAR DIARY
or
INTELLIGENCE SUMMARY.

(Erase heading not required.)

Instructions regarding War Diaries and Intelligence Summaries are contained in F. S. Regs., Part II. and the Staff Manual respectively. Title pages will be prepared in manuscript.

Place	Date	Hour	Summary of Events and Information	Remarks and references to Appendices
TOURCOING	8th to 14th Dec. 1918.		Training was carried out on the same lines as during the previous week. On Dec. 10th at 11 a.m. the Division was inspected at MOUVEAUX by the Corps Commander. Brigade Platoon and Grand Mounting Competitions took place on the 13th and 14th. The Battalion was third in the Platoon Competition (A Coy competing) and first in the Grand Mounting Competition ("B" Coy.). The Divisional Football Tattoo was reported in the PLACE DE LA REPUBLIQUE TOURCOING on Dec. 9th. Several football matches played. On Dec. 10th a party of N.C.Os and men travelled to LILLE. 22 men sent home for demobilisation.	Mr.
do.	15th to 21st Dec. 1918.		Training on hyper cycled and on Friday a route march was carried out. Parties of Officers, N.C.Os and men visited BRUGES on Dec. 16th. On Dec. 20th 4 Officers proceeded to BRUSSELS to attend fete. 20 men minus sent despatched for demobilisation. Educational classes continued. Lectures delivered on ALSACE-LORRAINE. Battalion attended truces.	Mr.

Army Form C. 2118.

WAR DIARY
or
INTELLIGENCE SUMMARY.

(Erase heading not required.)

Instructions regarding War Diaries and Intelligence Summaries are contained in F. S. Regs., Part II. and the Staff Manual respectively. Title pages will be prepared in manuscript.

Place	Date	Hour	Summary of Events and Information	Remarks and references to Appendices
TOURCOING	22nd Dec. 1918	6.31"	Training continued as before except that men attention was paid to enforcing or maintaining "off-rouse". A route march was held on 27th Dec. In addition to usual weekly statistics & claims on book-keeping, has begun. Several details were sent to the Battalion Recreation Room and a return on "Ammunition" attached. Preparations for Christmas were made on a much larger scale than has been possible before. Special dinners were held for the men on Xmas Day and the battalion attended the Pantomime "Cinderella" on Dec 27th. A Christmas Day forget was given for the Ned Recreation Room. Prizes were given, and the prizes were won by "D" Coy. Competition who were Keen.	Mu.

Mu.
md Sour
Lt. Col.
Cmdg 10th IKSR. 2 I.

Confidential

War Diary
of
10th (S) Bn Highland Light
Infantry
for
January 1917.

(6392) Wt. W6192/P875 1,500,000 4/18 McA & W Ltd (E 2815) Forms W3091/4   Army Form W.3091.

Cover for Documents.

Nature of Enclosures.

Notes, or Letters written,

WAR DIARY
or
INTELLIGENCE SUMMARY

Army Form C. 2118.

Place	Date	Hour	Summary of Events and Information	Remarks and references to Appendices
TOURCOING	1-1-19 – 3/1/19		Companies were billeted at TOURCOING on 1st and 2nd Jan. On 2/1/19 a Battalion parade was held under the Adjutant at 0900. Preparation for move to MARCQ. Battalion moved to MARCQ on 3/1/19. Bn. H.Q. No 31 RUE DE MENIN.	Ap
MARCQ	4/1/19 – 5/1/19		Settling down to billets. Men inspected by Join Bde. Agricultural Cmt at BONDUES.	Ap
"	6/1/19 – 12/1/19		During the week training took the form of 1 hour holding training and 1 hour Lectures. On 7/1/19 the B.G.C. inspected companies in turn. A Coy Fire marching Rules R Coy Musketry Rules — Arms Drill C an Stamp Kit inspection. During the week the battalion was billeted at BONDUES. The following decoration was announced on 12/1/19 Belgian Croix de Guerre No 41088 Sgt. J.F. BARKER, No 581 Pte. J. McMAHON. During the week 1 officer — 76 O.R. absentees.	Ap

Army Form C. 2118.

WAR DIARY
or
INTELLIGENCE SUMMARY.
(Erase heading not required.)

Instructions regarding War Diaries and Intelligence Summaries are contained in F.S. Regs., Part II. and the Staff Manual respectively. Title pages will be prepared in manuscript.

Place	Date	Hour	Summary of Events and Information	Remarks and references to Appendices
MARCQ	13/1/19 – 19/1/19		Coys were inspected daily on company & in a line to full marching order by C.O. on 16/1/19 a lecture on Imperial Policy by Rev. T.P. Williams. On 17/1/19 a football match officers V. Sergeants was played. 2 officers and 38 O.R. demobilised. Training continued on same lines as before.	Pm
"	20/1/19 – 26/1/19		Baths at BONDUES daily until 24/1/19. Another parade for Presentation of Ribbons but held under Capt. O WATT and Capt. J.A. SMITH M.C. Others were presented by Corps. Commander at ROUBAIX on 25/1/19. 4 officers and 107 O.R. demobilised. Training continues as before.	Pm
"	27/1/19 – 31/1/19		27th Lecture at BONDUES by hon. F.W. GILL on Travel and adventure in Egypt, Spain and England. 30th Baths at BONDUES. 31st No 246 Cpl/Sergt F. Hardie awarded M.S.M. 2 officers and 82 O.R. demobilised.	Pm

James Shirebo Major
for Lt. Col.
15 Coming 18th West L.I.

No. 45

3H.L.
4 sheets

Confidential

War Diary

of

10th/11th Durham Regiment Light Infantry

from 1 February 1919 to 28th February 1919.

(6392) Wt. W6192/P875 1,500,000 4/18 McA & W Ltd (E 2815) Forms W3091/4. Army Form W.3091.

Cover for Documents.

Nature of Enclosures.

Notes, or Letters written.

Army Form C. 2118.

WAR DIARY
or
INTELLIGENCE SUMMARY.
(Erase heading not required.)

Instructions regarding War Diaries and Intelligence Summaries are contained in F.S. Regs., Part II. and the Staff Manual respectively. Title pages will be prepared in manuscript.

Place	Date	Hour	Summary of Events and Information	Remarks and references to Appendices
MARCQ	1.2.19		1 hr Military Training and 1 hr Educational Training. 1 Officer & 32 other ranks demobilized.	
	2.2.19		Divine Service. 1 Officer & 16 other ranks demobilized.	
	3.2.19		1 hr each Mil. and Educational Training. 29 other ranks demobilized.	
	4.2.19		Lecture by R.T.O. Educational Officer, subject "South Africa" & 1 hr Mil. Training.	
	5.2.19		1 hr each Military and Educational Training.	
	6.2.19		1 hr Educational Training. The Bn. on visit to RONCHES. 25 O.R. demobilized.	
	7.2.19		Lecture at ROUBAIX by Mr Hollins Beelin, subject "Strategical Surgery" and 1 hour Mil. and Educational Training. 1 Officer and 30 other ranks demobilized.	
	8.2.19		Lecture at ROUBAIX by Earl of Derby, subject "He would share for human Demonstran" 1 Officer & 6 other ranks demobilized. 1 hr each Mil. and Educational Training.	
	9.2.19		Divine Service. 1 Officer and 50 other ranks demobilized.	
	10.2.19		1 hr Educational and 1 hr Military Training. 1 Officer and 4 other ranks demobilized.	
	11.2.19		1 hr each Military and Educational Training.	
	12.2.19		1 hr each Military and Educational Training.	
	13.2.19		1 hr each Military and Educational Training. 3 Officers demobilized.	
	14.2.19		1 hr Educational Training. Draft of other ranks reported (but ch.) by Capt. T.M. WALKER. This draft consist of "1916" enlisted men for transfer to Army of Occupation.	
	15.2.19		1 hr Educational Training. Billets inspected by Army officer.	
	16.2.19		Divine Service.	
	17.2.19		Educational Training. 1 hr. The H.A shifted to 139 RUE DE LILLE.	
	18.2.19		Educational Training. 1 hr. Settling down in new H.Q.	
	19.2.19		1 hr each Mil. and Educational Training. S.M.M. 355144 2/6Lt. W. KENNEDY awarded M.M.	
	20.2.19		1 hr each Mil. and Educational Training. Draft for Army of Occupation inspected by B.G.C.	

Army Form C. 2118.

Army Form C. 2118.

WAR DIARY
INTELLIGENCE SUMMARY.
(Erase heading not required.)

Instructions regarding War Diaries and Intelligence Summaries are contained in F. S. Regs., Part II. and the Staff Manual respectively. Title pages will be prepared in manuscript.

Place	Date	Hour	Summary of Events and Information	Remarks and references to Appendices
MARCQ	21/3/19 -22/3/19		2 hrs Military Training. Skirmy Drill, Handling of Arms, Guard mounting, all Bullets inspected on 22nd by Commdg Officer.	MM
	23/3/19		Divine Service.	MM
	24/3/19 -25/3/19		2 hrs Military Training. Skirmy Drill and Musketry (146 range)	MM
	25/3/19		1 hr Military Training. The Bn was billeted in BONDUES.	MM
	26/3/19		2 hrs Military Training. Skirmy Drill, Guard mounting and musketry. 1 Officer recognizing.	MM

[signature]

LT-COL
COMDG. 10TH HIGHRS LI

War Diary

10th Bn Highland L.I.

March 1919

Army Form C. 2118.

WAR DIARY
or
INTELLIGENCE SUMMARY.
(Erase heading not required.)

Instructions regarding War Diaries and Intelligence Summaries are contained in F. S. Regs., Part II and the Staff Manual respectively. Title pages will be prepared in manuscript.

Place	Date	Hour	Summary of Events and Information	Remarks and references to Appendices
MARCQ	1-3-19		1th Meeting Training. Clearing & inspection of Billets. 1 N.C.O. discharged	11/3/19
	2-3-19		Divine Service. Change to summer time. 2 O.R. discharged	11/3/19
	3-3-19		2th Military Training. 14 O.R. discharged	11/3/19
	4-3-19		all men not on fatigues unearthing tents	11/3/19
	5-3-19		all other ranks on fatigues. Burying stores on	11/3/19
	6-3-19		Bathing Parade. Reserve of S.A.A. and Bombs to MENIN and LINSELLES	11/3/19
	7-3-19		2th Military Training	11/3/19
	8-3-19		fatigues cleaning out inspection of Billets	11/3/19
	9-3-19		Divine Service	11/3/19
	10-3-19		Removal of bombs and stores to PETIT OUDENARDE. 1 O.R. discharged	11/3/19
	11-3-19		2th Military Training	11/3/19
	12-3-19		2th Military Training	11/3/19
	13-3-19		Bathing Parade	11/3/19
	14-3-19		2th Military Training	11/3/19
	15-3-19		Fatigues clearing out inspection of tents	11/3/19
	16-3-19		Divine Service	11/3/19
	17-3-19		1½ hr Military training ½ hr lecture	11/3/19
	18-3-19		1½ hr Military training ½ hr lecture	11/3/19
	19-3-19		1½ hr Military training ½ hr lecture	11/3/19
	20-3-19		Bathing Parade	11/3/19
	21-3-19		1½ hr Military training ½ hr lecture	11/3/19
	22-3-19		Draft reported to 16th Bn #2 L.I. 2nd Army. 1 Officer discharged	11/3/19
	23-3-19		Divine Service.	11/3/19

WAR DIARY
or
INTELLIGENCE SUMMARY.
(Erase heading not required.)

Army Form C. 2118.

Instructions regarding War Diaries and Intelligence Summaries are contained in F. S. Regs., Part II. and the Staff Manual respectively. Title pages will be prepared in manuscript.

Place	Date	Hour	Summary of Events and Information	Remarks and references to Appendices
MARCQ	24/3/19		Cleaning up, instructing to recruits	A/H
	25/3/19		Cleaning up, instructing to recruits	A/H
	26/3/19		Battalion moved to PETIT OUDENARDE	A/H
PETIT OUDENARDE	27/3/19		Arranging Alms and Billets	A/H
	28/3/19		3 Officers and 5 other ranks demobilized (4 residues)	A/H
	29/3/19		Routine Work at PETIT OUDENARDE	A/H
	30/3/19			A/H
	31/3/19			A/H

A.R. Sanders Capt.
for O.C. 10th A.&S.H.

SECRET

96/47

36.L
3 sheets

War Diary
for
April 1919
of
10th/11th Bn. Highland Light
Infantry.

(6392) Wt. W6192/P875 1,500,000 4/18 McA & W Ltd (E 2815) Forms W3091/4.   Army Form W.3091.

Cover for Documents.

Nature of Enclosures.

Notes, or Letters written.

Army Form C. 2118.

WAR DIARY
INTELLIGENCE SUMMARY.
(Erase heading not required.)

Place	Date	Hour	Summary of Events and Information	Remarks and references to Appendices
PETIT OUDENARDE	1-4-19 to 30.4.19		During the month the batt: has been located at PETIT OUDENARDE and the days have been spent in ordinary routine work. The arranging Machinery Shows etc. for matches Baths at HERSEAUX were much used & useful. On the 4th 1 W.O. and 3 men went out from duty at BISSEGHEM against flying mines unknown on 16th as the outcome of the incident. On the 5th a party made by Mainstay to TOURNAI to witness the wrecking to Railway & branches. A communication from XV Corps regarding the delay in leave to England and the loss of available time of terminated in the same manner was laid before the men. The reasoning of leave has tended to reduce discontent as the delays in Demobilization. During the month, one Officer and eight other ranks were sent for demobilization (4 of the other ranks being men who had re-engaged for two years.)	

[signature] Major Comdg. 10th Highl. L.I.

30/4/19

CONFIDENTIAL

37.L

WAR DIARY
of
10th/11th High. L.I.
for
May 1919.

(6392) Wt. W6192/P875 1,500,000 4/18 McA & W Ltd (E 2815) Forms W3091/4.   Army Form W.3091.

Cover for Documents.

Nature of Enclosures.

Notes, or Letters written.

WAR DIARY
or
INTELLIGENCE SUMMARY.

(Erase heading not required.)

Army Form C. 2118.

Place	Date	Hour	Summary of Events and Information	Remarks and references to Appendices
PETIT AUDENARDE	1-5-19		For the month the Battn. has remained in billets in PETIT AUDENARDE awaiting instructions to proceed to U.K. Owing to the reduction in the cadre establishment 1 Officer and 9 other ranks were sent forward for demobilisation. During the month eight other ranks rejoined from the Luxemburg Armée d'Occupation Batt. and in return 1916 men Category A1 men were transferred to 16th H.L.I. 29th During the month eight sightseeing trips to OSTEND and BRUSSELS took place.	29th 29th
	31-5-19			

2/6/19.

M. Marsh Lieut Col of Comp.
10th Argyll L.I.

Secret

War Diary
of
10th Highland Light
Infantry
from
1st to 14th June 1919

Final

Army Form C. 2118.

WAR DIARY
or
INTELLIGENCE SUMMARY.
(Erase heading not required.)

Place	Date	Hour	Summary of Events and Information	Remarks and references to Appendices
PETIT AUDENARDE	1/6/19			
	13/6/19		The basis of this Bn remained in billets in PETIT AUDENARDE during the period and were exchanged preparing and training for move to demobilization and the cadre proceeded to Southampton & and to AALANDRE on 14th June, the & cadre consisting of 2 Officers and 13 men, the & others waiting to proceed to France.	

W.M. Macpherbell Major
10 A.L.I.

www.ingramcontent.com/pod-product-compliance
Lightning Source LLC
Chambersburg PA
CBHW081447160426
43193CB00013B/2404